Affection

Other books by Lynn Hard

Dancing on the Drainboard (1992)
Australia Suite (1998)
The Unused Portion (2013)
Poems New & Neglected (2016)

Affection

LYNN HARD

Drawings by Garry Shead

ETT IMPRINT
Exile Bay

This edition published by ETT Imprint, Exile Bay 2022

ETT IMPRINT
PO Box R1906
Royal Exchange NSW 1225
Australia

ISBN 978-1-922698-02-5 (Limited edition hardback)
ISBN 978-1-922473-70-7 (paperback)
ISBN 978-1-922473-71-4 (ebook)

Cover: Garry Shead, *Love in the Kitchen*, oil on canvas 1995; courtesy the artist

Designed by Tom Thompson

For Aurora Ferrante
Whose only fault is a fondness for my poetry.

CONTENTS

Affection

My partner of 30 years
has fallen asleep on the couch
turned away from the television,
a large, green rectangle
of a golf tournament,
people walking around in a painting.
She doesn't see
the putt roll past the hole
that changes all the numbers
on the leaderboard.
She sleeps on
and neither of us knows
what other parts of the schedule she missed
before the golf appeared.

And in the other large rectangle of that room
another nocturnal creature,
the birthmarked moon,
rises, wakeless,
to its place
its expression
hard to read.
Perhaps it has a cry
or a call
but at that distance
amid all the chatter of the stars and other night things
cannot be heard,
cannot wake her,
while I,
who can,
will not
break her dream.

For a Friend Going Home

To Spiro Petroulos

So you're going back to Greece
and, of course, you know
most of us would like a return
to Greece:
the mountains well placed,
land inset with bits of sea,
grey green olive groves
corn rowing the hills,
islands littered about
oracled temples on each,
around the next bush
a myth,
the journey ending at Athens
and the Acropolis
that colonnaded height
gleaming like a great musical
instrument.

But,
when you arrive
there will be a stubble
of scaffolding
across the marble fronts,
scruffy archeologists and brickies
preserving the ruin.
Just as they are
in Washington
and a few other places, patching,
fencing off, boarding up,
conserving what's left.

I mean, anyone can build something new,
but it takes a real handyman
to be doing the most important work:
pursuing the repair
of our monuments,

like some constellate
dog
pursues a rolling planet
through all time
to bring back what's left of it
to its owner.

Experimental Films

for Garry & Rose

No 1

There was a place,
near where I grew up,
where you could stand on the sidewalk
and look in
on people dining elegantly,
well dressed,
correct in their cutlery,
cuff linked against linen napkins

and,
as a boy,
I knew they were not of my time.
The image in the window
as unattainable as
an empty chair at a nightclub table
between Cary Grant and Lauren Bacall.

And still,
when I watch a movie,
a bit of me is on the footpath
looking in at the past,
for all film is history
period pieces,
where I can observe
but not go.

No 2

If my family,
by that I mean my parents
and myself,
ever had a coat of arms
it would be
my mother and I
on either side
of a big rustic sign
saying “WELCOME TO WYOMING” or
“MONTANA” or wherever.
My father’s not there
because he’s taking the picture,
recording
multiple proofs
that we’d been around.

They went on to their retirement
and I went on to adultery
my image not present
in the thousands of slides
made on travels to places worn away
by endless others
and their light snatching cameras:
the biggest wine barrel in the world,
Bill Shakespeare’s house,
the Parthenon,
Mom and Dad at some once disputed barricade,
Mom and Dad and the tour guide at the Great Wall,
anywhere that you can’t see your house from.

All those slides in the house
when I went to clear it out
and 4 cans of Super 8 film
in a box with a projector,
standing erect like a little lion rampant, a
winch into the past
pulling up pictures of lost occasions,
Christmases, birthdays, graduations
that would have been important
if I had made anything of my life.
Unlike todays films,
these flicker
giving them a kind of diffidence
and believability.
With a yearning I seem to have always had
I went to the screen
to touch the actors,
the major characters in my life.
Running my fingers through the movie,
images dripping away,

I thought of that old song
about Don Quixote:
"A man with moonlight in his hands
has nothing there at all."

Attribution. From "To Each His Dulcinea"
Lyricist Joe Darion.

Farewell Animal

for W.B.Y.

Last night
in whatever sleep is
I wandered onto the set of **The Quiet Man**
where they were shooting my wake
and me Irish.
I was laid out in a room with whitewashed, rough plastered walls
like the inner chamber of a cloud.
The women of the village
piling up the scones and cakes
in a kind of ritual masonry,
pouring the tea from pots as earthen and thick
as the cottages they live in
mourning what they had got of me.
The men, by now spilling as much as they drink,
talking of someone whose name I didn't catch,
whilst I lay there
dreaming in my best clothes
aware I would never be in style again
or cause a current to flow differently,
but still content

knowing, with the only certitude
I can recall,
that the time I was about to spend
would not be wasted.

I woke
to find myself on a backlot
of avenues unravelling with weeds,
labelled with expatriate street signs
stocked with shabby, schizoid buildings
and scenery
piled like specimen slides:
a debris of life
on the cutting room floor.

A Fascination with the Queen of Spades

My impossibly old Grandmother,
the prosecuting attorney of my single digit years,
gave me 4 gifts:
a bible,
a pack of cards,
the rules of solitaire
and an introduction to the Queen of Spades:

that perfect faced lady
who always looked away
but was always there within the society of the deck,
became the elder sibling
to that only child

and the favourite performer
in years of shuffles,
deals
and games.

When I won
her expression never changed,
when I cheated
she reproved me

for seeking to alter
the unexpected entrances and exits
of she and her friends
as they elegantly obeyed and evaded
the restrictions of the game.

I listened
and gave up vandalism
for art.

At 82 I still play,
waiting for her to turn up

waiting for her nonchalance
her *honi soit qui mal y pense*

her resemblance to my grandmother
when she was young.

Lunching at Lucio's

for Lucio

I sit at a window table
in this fashionable restaurant
in a fashionable neighbourhood
made by a god
heavily influenced by Vermeer
and it's like being in an ideal
witness protection plan.
Aged bricks artfully piled make
up the buildings,
the grass in the nature strips are
green Wiltons
wearing the shade of mature trees
like a costly wrap
and a jacaranda
has dropped its petals
at the curved corner of a street
like mauve eyeshadow
on a stone eyelid.

In the restaurant
the starched white tables
stand on the dark tiles
like the nuns of Brittany

on the walls
everywhere are the paintings
of artists
influenced by the 20th century,
my century,
each a bit of an opening
onto Australia.
The food comes
and it is like a prisoner's
last meal.
A gustatory event
where individual tastes
stud my memory
like the sounds of the toccata in D.

The large bill paid,
I wait
as the evening begins
to shut down the town,
for a taxi
to return me
to the suburb where I have lived
years of tax evasion
and dodgy charitable donations
pottering
among the guilty pleasures
of all the things
I might finish
some day.

Rae Desmond Jones & the Maquis

Had Rae Desmond Jones,
the mayor of an Australian town,
lived in 1943
he would have recognized a country like France
occupied by a foreign power,
governed by local bureaucrats
who'd finally found their kind of ally:
one who believed in rules against difference,
but not against menace.

Rae,
like the french resistants,
left his own
real life
to oppose the suburban boche
and their Vichy lackies.

Oh, he'd been practicing as a resistant
for most of his life
writing his poems,
his books,
teaching/talking to students,
reasoning
in his soft way,
taking pleasure in a laughing sort of sedition.

Protecting, not really progress,
but the process.

Aware that life
is not a matter of advances
but one of defending outposts
and he did that,
accepting the occasional wins
and frequent tactical withdrawals
as routine
just as in France
the liberation
ended only the latest war.

Retirement
didn't finish his resistance.
He wrote more words,
talked more talk
until, under siege by the inevitable,
he staged his last sorties
and retreats
expending the final stratagem.

This Christmas
I won't find a poem
slipped under my door
or be visited
by a tall
black hatted man
with a bottle of red
in his rucksack
or hear more of what happened in the Australian movie
before I came in

and there'll be one less
at any barricade
you care to name.

Reading Paul Celan

for Simon Sharwood

All I know is hearsay,
my poems written by a bystander
seldom even, a person of interest
because
no pogrom
ever dismissed
my closed doors
to drag me by my lapels
out
in the disordered street
to watch
the contents of my photo albums
burn.
Leaving me undocumented
with only desperate recollections
to ensure
that I am not forgot.
a student
whose homework
was eaten by a beast.

Bush Fire

The great unfairness
spent the night in my garden
making the normally easy air
difficult,
surrounding all with a horizon
like a bloody bandage.

The australian bush burned
not too far from me
the vast act of vandalism
breaking
every rural heart
as their unwarranted optimisms
curled
and blackened.

Some of them
my friends,
who
may have made a mistake
to go beyond good reception
to where only the specialized
animals and plants are,
will return
to renovate the ruins
and find the views they so admire
and others will question their wisdom in doing so
but not I, for don't they have as much right
in this matter
as the fire?

How Do We Know

for Elissa Baxter

How do we know
that the night's
precise apportioning of light and dark
exact spacing between stars
the time tabling of comets
what stands in the foreground or at the back
is not a great mistake
or series of mistakes
a plan
whose moment of failure
is yet to come?

That the night
is not an ivy of stars
covering the cracked and bent walls of buildings
occupied by transients
unaware of their original purpose

and that anyone
under the universe
looking up
can hold a misconception
and be blameless

while anyone outside
looking down
is either right
or shameless

Singin' in the Rain

I ran into Gene Kelly the other night:
singin' and dancin' in the rain
norfolk jacket drenched,
a pair of sodden wing-tips
kickin' water around like it was in the way,
really taking the mickey out of the weather.
Bonkers,
I thought.
And so did a cop,
all caped, spit shiny black,
like the Hun on a war poster,
who came along to end the wet, soft shoe.

So Gene
shrugged, turned
and strode away from the law
toward a sunny day

handing me his unused umbrella.
as we passed,
softly saying:
"Watch out for him."

For a long instant
I wanted to follow him up Franklin
past my door
to wherever he was going.

But,
I needed my smokes
and the cop was looking at me,
so I walked on
into the rain that rattled the pavement
like fingers drumming on a restaurant table
where the service is poor.

I got my pack of "Mahouts"
and headed home another way.
Gene's umbrella
proved to be most useful

and I still have it today.

Visit

for the Irvings

Tuesday,
they were here when I got home,
the writer and his family
presences
natural
in their positions in the lounge room
like a George Segal construction.

For a few days
they would occupy the far end
of the hen run
that Helen and I
wander in
hiding from our pecking order,
losing our eggs.

Readings, interviews
were arranged,
unnatural deposits of culture
mined
the children creating their own pac-man
sub-sets

and interacting
with Helen's new dog,
a Shelty puppy:
perpetually bewildered,
scuttling from person to person

as if seeking news
of some important event:
a declaration of war,
a visit by the Doge,
the closing of the kitchen.

We started with the treasures of my cellar,
which didn't take long,
and moved
through the ordinary vin
on to bottles brought to meals
by people who don't drink
as I would bring food
to a toucan.

Then
the records:
I drape the jewelry of jazz
over them
obsidian collars of LPs,
ear plugs of disc,
the horologes of cassettes

Johnny Hodges,
Johnny Irving,
2 kids,
a dog,
all
(with Queen Adelaide sitting in)
play a piece
that doesn't admit to
arrangement.

Thursday
and the windows of their car
begin to fill up
with sleeping bags,
anoraks,
lolly packets,
accumulated booty
and Friday
when I get home
the house is quiet.
The dog,
for lack of anything better to do,
is chasing its tail
on the lawn
like a tone arm at the end of a record,
an old sum
is displayed on the stereo,
LP covers lie prone
scattered as if an outrage
had taken place.

There are no echoes,
no aural mementos of puppy-girl
understandings,
if these walls could talk
they wouldn't,
just a sense of dilution
that something has been removed
leaving it not as
silent
as it was.

I Wish I Could Copy the Poppy

I wish I could copy
the poppy
and only live in the spring
folding my arms,
a brown study,
during earth's chastening;

but I must be four seasoned
like the penalized evergreen
content to shingle wooden flowers
to give to an occasional Proserpine.

At Saqqara

At Saqqara,
without a warrant,
they broke into Wahtye's tomb,
silent for four and a half thousand years,
going through everything,
seizing his lap top,
the contents of his filing cabinets
and surprising
this dignified official,
member of many boards,
asleep
in his humble
plank dressing gown.

I spent today
with my phone turned off,
building
my unpublished haystacks of needles,
binding
my paper cuts,
surrounded by the carefully shelved
collections of my interests
and soon
I will make my way
down a long corridor
to my shuttered bedchamber
and lay myself down
in my most private
and personal cot
rolling over
and pressing my nose
against the grindstone of my pillow,
hoping to catch
4500 winks.

Summer Evening

I wish
the cicadas
would finish their renovations,
sell
and move on

leaving
us two
to quietly continue
counting the insect stars.

Thoughts on a Chinese Grave in Braidwood

Lonely, lonely
this place.
No one is family.
No one is known.
All
pieces from broken sets.
Lonely land
not many plants,
not many animals,
unsheltered,
untended,
unwritten,
without legend,
exposed,
unshaped.
Not like my home province
where the landscape is like opera,
scenes come into sight:
a narrow fall of water
like a scholar's beard;
along the bank
willows wash their hair in the wind
and the green terraces of rice
step up the hills
like a great man's mind.

Lonely
so that only the work is good,
understandable,
just.

My people said to me:
"Why do you go there
and place yourself at the bottom
losing your place here?"
and I said,
or I hope I said
"It isn't the place that's the problem,
it's the length of the stay."

In my province
in China
you are born
and your past begins

here in this lonely place
there is nothing but foreign space
and tomorrow.

Coupling

At first it was sex
In strange positions,
on location, under studio lights.
In between changing the sheets
you said "Don't let this make you think
we're a couple, 'cause we're not.
I'm not shaping my life to yours."

I nodded like the Alsatian
in the back of the car
and tried it with one foot on the floor.
When we finished I asked you to marry me,
you said no.

Later, after three defacto years
more like MacBeth and MacDuff
than Lunt and Fontanne,
you postulated children, mentioned marriage
and I invoked a clause in our original
contract and said no.

I live with someone else
and have wholly lost track of you
but in that matter of our lives
I'm sure you had the right of it:
we're never couples,
there is no position strange enough
to make us fit.

Cameo

a Lorca

If you shoot at me
I will shoot back
If you kill me
I will not die
If you abandon me
I will follow you

You can only go as far
as the border of our little cameo
where there is the smallest of defaced moons
and perhaps a mountain
or is it a house
and the white wave of the stone
that is hard to see as water

We are here in this heirloom brooch
a bit art, mostly accident
both always the same distance between
just about to leave
just about to speak

Probably the clasp will break
and our minor rock
fall over the edge of the world
to tumble
endlessly
endlessly
endlessly
you no farther
I no nearer

How Far Has Light Fallen

How far has this light fallen
and how long has it been falling
spilled by some busy star hurrying
along its numbered tram line losing
more and more day
until it reaches the dark
that gives night its name

Les Murray

Les
thought so much
saw every issue
but looking at them
from around
the warped and faded walls
of poor and abandoned
didn't always see
every side

I think
he eventually would
have gotten to every side
but before he could
he came to that inevitable sad ending
that leaves us all
unfinished

I'm the same age as Les
living among ripe bananas and
death notices.
With each loss
whether they be friends, acquaintances or foes
the cast of characters
shrinks
making it harder
to play the play
I've always known.
I was dealing a hand of solitaire
when I heard about Les
and I dedicated it to him,
I won.

Rides

To get to any of the National Parks
my parents were obsessed by
you had to travel,
at night,
through a flat, desolate land
past darkened gas stations,
rows of tattered tourist cabins
and ruined buildings
where only the stone fireplaces and chimneys
remained.

It was the best part of the trip.
I watched
from my position on the back seat
which only I
and whatever camping equipment wouldn't fit on the roof rack
or trunk
shared,
imagining who had inhabited these places my window went by,
why they were abandoned,
who or what
had emptied or destroyed them.
They were like vacant settings
waiting to be occupied
by the stories
I loved to read.

In the same trip,
I'm in the back of a taxi
on the way to the airport
drifting in traffic
when
on the footpath next to me
a young, slender woman
dressed in blue jeans,
white shirt
and runners
skips down some steps

and turns to the left
her arms up
fastening a long ponytail
behind her head as she walks.
At the same pace
as the cab
she moves along the street
and I think there is room
beside her,
then she reaches a corner
and turns away from me
diminishing up one of the many chains
in the vast hauberk
of interlocking avenues
that is Sydney.

Later
an even older me,
in a young relative's car,
follows a familiar
route
to yet another parking space.
All the vehicles
have their lights on,
as if it were dark.
A park goes by the window
and I see a single kite,
perhaps the last of a flock,
struggling in a tree:
an answer
whose problem
has blown away.

Gibbous in Banjine Street

for Mark and Jan O'Connor

Like a one-day cricket ball
in the 49th over
the dis-rounded moon
rises
above Banjine Street
its light
slowly filling up the block
like a thermometer
telling the temperature backward.

The light
whittled from the orb,
falls on
cats
who slip it on like something
more comfortable;
writers
recreating perpendicular noons
in Tuscany;
and the work-a-day trees
of the sun-drowned front gardens
who use it
in their time off,
to cut
themselves
flattering silhouettes.

Hubris

Faustus, more brazen than Wittenberg's walls,
conjured up a soul, a devil
and bartered them to each other
in return for one, Helen,
whose mouth was a Deity.
The Gods, interrupting their game of tennis,
came down to punish this lack of piety
and pricked his bladder of vanity
with a needle of belief.
Faustus, like a neurotic retort
conceiving itself to be empty,
hurtled off and shattered against those same walls.

When I See the Isolate Stars

When I see the isolate stars
bristling and needled with brightness
I wonder if once
all this darkness was star
and has been slowly
blacked and gouged away
'til now each one
is locked in its separate position
within the feudatory night
unable to move except to march
in close order drill
from one bayonet
to the next.

Thoughts on parade:
Is burning the same as living?

Susanna and the Elders and Thomas Hart Benton

Old Tom Benton
knew,
it's about prurience
and prurience needs to be real
so that gal in his painting
could be from the next farm over
(the marks of her underwear
still evident on her skin)
or cousin Harmon's wife
on a visit.
The renaissance Susies
were made
to be spied upon
but Tom's Suzy
is secret
and self-absorbed,
defenceless.

As a representative
of most men,
I've liked looking at naked women
since before
the rutting urge came on me:
exciting because it was sneaky.
I guess
a lot of it
is the clothes.
I think
men and women must have

worked together
on clothes,
maybe theatre
started with the costumes,
putting them on
and taking them off
like the dance
of a signaler
and the coloured flags.
Unclothed animals
with their seasonal
matings
don't seem to do it.
Peeking's
just for us
gaining an advantage,
intimacy without an interview
or the possibility
of not getting the job.

The story of Susanna and the elders
is not religion,
that's why the protestants
didn't put it in their bible,
although I could easily imagine
a tv evangelist being involved.
No, it's not about religion,
it goes quite aways past the steeple, the parking lot,
the collection plate, the nave.
And if you're wondering
about the 2 old voyeurs:
they didn't get hung for prurience,
but the crime that came next.

Anniversaries

This might be (no,
is, probably)
an anniversary
of something in my life
or yours
maybe I met what's-her-name
on this very day
a long time ago
or maybe it's when she left me
(no, hold on, I left her!)
when I lived in Melbourne.
Or your mother died,
I think in 1968,
an event so mysterious to me,
with both my parents running
like generators:
a normal noise out back
that stops the milk from spoiling
and keeps the lights on,
that I never asked you about it.

I know,
what say we limit it to beginnings?
Just the openings,
no end games,
when everything's a surprise
and on the floor of your personal stock
exchange
it's a bull market.
Yeah, let's do that
let's agree to a beginning next week
right here.

Yes,
this would be a good place
if the weather's nice,
with the grass and trees,
the flowers in their jars,
the thumbnail sketches on the stones
just you and me.

I'd like another anniversary.

How Shy

How shy
this moon in a land of mountains and trees
diffident
standing at the back
behind the crowds of branches
and the shrugged shoulders of hills
spending the evening
gathering its nerve
jumping
to gain my attention
holding up its disc
at the best angle it can get
the only part of the night
that is not silhouette.

Barbra Streisand

Why didn't I ever meet Barbra Streisand?
met lot's of others,
but she stayed in the darkened doorways of my speakers
our relationship purely hearsay,
but no one walking outside,
encumbered with all the dimensions,
ever so sustained a note,
ever lay in wait with me
to delay time,
holding it up
for a season or two.

And the photographs
on those albums
of her wry admittance
that these are her mother's clothes
(arms akimbo)
like Dorothy
grown up
with her evenings free
and a maturer taste
in shoes.

And I claim that she lent a style
to the clusters of vacant rooms
and the clusters of occupants
who'd nailed
copies of Van Gogh's drawbridge
and Chagall posters
to the walls,
with literary documents of plea bargains
spread over all those coffee tables.

You may differ,

but I'm too old
and it's too late to argue,
caught in this coda that's
all vibrato
and regret,
that at the end of my time
I never met
Barbra Streisand

and infinitely worse,
perhaps,
she never met her either.

Fall

for Grant Caldwell

Affixing
all the red leaves
to the trees
is meticulous
and time consuming
like shingling
against a deadline.

But,
if they come from
inside
they are
easy,
off hand,
nonchalant
like distributing
samples of something
as casual
as beauty.

Jazz, the Movie

In 1941 Orson Welles hired Duke Ellington to work on a film about the history of jazz. Duke wrote some music, but the film was never made.

Ah, but it might have been.

Suppose,
warm weather in New Orleans.
It's late in a turn of the century day
and shadows chevron the streets.

Imagine,
a tall black man coming out of Bolden's barber shop:
silk shirt,
sleeve garters,
tight, pin-stripe trousers
and, today, a planter's hat.

Put in,
2 women to attend him
dressed to invite more speculation
than most at that time.
One carries Buddy's coat,
for this is the great Buddy Bolden,
the other has his trumpet
in a red felt bag.

Watch
them walk away
toward Storyville
and a planked building with outside stairs
meant for drinking and seeing things
through a glass darkly
where tonight Buddy will play like he dresses.

Retrieve
a mood from one of your best days,
give it to him,
and you'll still be short.

At the swinging doors,
the women go into the used beer interior
looking for early friends.
Buddy takes his horn and his coat upstairs
to practice alone.

See
the trumpet polished 'til it's precious,
the valves oiled like hair triggers.
Buddy doesn't play scales
or tease out arrangements;
Buddy doesn't practice restrictions,
he practices manumission
28 bars of the purest
improvisation
to still the dissonance
in the room below.

This is where Duke Ellington's History of Jazz
plays out
with "The best 28 bars" he ever wrote
and then he lost it!
This is all Orson got for his money
and the movie that was never made.

But, let's take it a bit further
roll the evening forward
the big upstairs room crowded and hot,
the piano player dripping sweat on the keys,
a glistening Buddy on the stand
calling the numbers,
smiling and nodding at friends in the crowd
then raising the brightest horn
and blowing hard
straightening out that coiled
and pressured knot in his head
until it's plaited into its original shape
and alive in the air.

Visualize
the damp audience
shortsleeved, jacketed, cleavage,
tight rolled cigarettes, cheap jewelry,
some talking,
some drinking,
some rapt,
all necessary.

Nearly all black,
except a white sailor or two
and, maybe, in the back
a jew from a touring minstrel show
named Jolson.
Witnesses to magic
a historic performance
that will enlarge in the telling
like the unrecorded deeds
of our childhood heroes.

Finish
your drink
and move off into the New Orleans night
warmer than most place's days,
beginning
to forget
the sequence of tunes,
names of the sidemen.

Hope
that one day
as the barbershop door
closes behind you
on the cut hair
and blunted razors
you'll have a place
to find
your own reveille to blow
and let all that's gordian
go.

Headlines

"Night Storm Savages North Coast Town"

I made this boat
shaped most of the hull
bought the rest
and made it fit.

When I'm in it
each bit that comes to hand
lets me relive
the triumphs of its construction

and every repair,
new piece of gear,
repainting
is a tinkering with myself.

Last night
I was out north of Yamba
watching the stars
and taking the slaps of the sea

abused by the waves
yet not abused,
there's a certain satisfaction
in observing the sea and the boat
performing their duties.

On the ocean at night
without the moon
it's black above
and it's black below

and the stars
are near
close and still
so that they seem on the edge of explaining themselves.

I've often thought
that this is how it was
when people believed in Zeus and Juno:
it's what comes from being too familiar with the stars.

It was about 8
when the sea speeded up
and then at half-past
the wind seemed to take a personal interest in the boat and me.

On a hunch
I headed away from shore
and just before 9
the storm took the stars

the clouds black plumes
and the wind at us
violent and screaming
like funeral horses gone mad.

The water in and out of my clothes,
sail dropped like a poor excuse,
the boat and me
our only hope.

It was bad
but we made it
back to a sunny day
of make and mend at the wharf.

I understand they weren't so lucky
inland.
The little town of Tucabia
lost 45 roofs, 8 houses and a church.

They would have been well into *The World's Funniest Home Videos*
when the power went.
Likely
they'll re-run it.

Tucabia's a farming community
and I'm sorry for their trouble
as they grieve for their wrecked houses and barns
among their nonchalant animals.

That grief and the stars and the storm;
that they build something to lose,
that they mourn its loss
that the church went first
is curious.

"APEC Flexes Its Trade Muscles"

How have we come to this?
Barter
on the front page
of our mornings
a photo of transient leaders
clutching the rail of their ferry ride
abashed, puzzled faces
behind their Punch and Judy waves
not
beyond their depth
but lost in the shallows
surrounded
by a thin lipped horizon.

Are all the constitutions
written on the back of balance sheets?
As if "balance"
were the object.
What shopkeeper
could survive on "balance"?

It's caveat emptor
instead of Dieu et mon Droit
and the politicians
in their glossy hard hats
tour the factory floor
walking amongst the foremen
like women
who come and go
talking of Fats Domino.

Let's be clear here.
We defenestrated the fops
and their words
copperplated on foolscap
in exchange for longer trading hours.
They had the church
we short term interest rates.

Listen,
you get your "freedom"
not from principles
but by atavistic accident
like Cratchett losing his situation,
like meteors missing the moon
and you know what I say?
The only good ejaculation
is the one that comes too soon.

APEC

The Poems One Writes in Old Age

Of course
it's the same old thing
and yes,
one shouldn't write whole books of poems about one joke;
where's the scenery,
the song,
the witty graffiti scrawled on all the walls,
the mythic year drawn and quartered into seasons,
love coming
on the page,
disappearing
into photo albums.

But, can't you see
from all those elegant messages
slipped under your door,
like light from a brighter room,
how much I still want to please you
how hard it is,
how frightened I am
and can't you see
how brave I am?

Now

An entry for the contest to determine the inscription to be placed over the entrance to the Widener Library at Harvard ran: "This is not the library, the library is inside." It did not win.

A tall Scaffolding
has been rolled into the foyer of the library
so that the lights in the ceiling
can be changed.
The diagonal bars
make it look like a gigantic "N",
the maintenance staff in coloured jump suits
festooning it
into the first
illuminated letter
of the vast collection
that lies behind it.

That "N"
is the first letter
of the first word
which is "Now",
which is what everything is
until the latecomers
call it then:
from cuneiform grain inventories
to hieroglyph boasts
to attempts to catch God's eye with gold leaf

to cave doodlings
to German bibles that seemed
a good idea at the time to
leaflets dropped from planes
to first editions of so what
to all the best ideas so far
to overdue notices
that remind me
that "Now" is only loaned and
I must not keep Montaigne,
Basho,
Popular Mechanics,
Justine
or *Dancing on the Drainboard*
too long.

January 6, 2021

How dare this tawdry,
fat man
with his artificial hair
and dyed skin
whose only accomplishment
is to cheat others
of their wealth

trash
one of the last things I believe in,
entice the scum of the internet
to attack the rights of man,
violate the truths
we hold to be self evident,
smear their vileness
across the marble nobility
of our best,

doubt the decades
of rectitude
that have refined
our elections
so that we are all
given a place
and a voice
in our now
and what is to be?

How dare
this little, unclean
creature
and the crepuscular
mediocrities
who attend him
stain
the enormous,
profound thoughts
of those whose
giganticism
casts not shadow
but light,
a distillation
of this country's
finest
whose example
excludes
this pudgy tyrant
and his followers
from what
all those of worth
have sacrificed
and fought for.

Will no one stand
with me and forbid
them what they
have forfeited:
the right to a place
among the honest,
the honorable,
the rational,
the decent.

Printed in Australia
AUHW010230280222
360187AU00006B/9

9 781922 473707